TEMPEST

Poetry for Earthly Renewal

edited by
TERRY HERMSEN

in collaboration with
EARLY INTERVAL
&
ROAR (REGIONAL OHIO ACTION for RESILIENCE)

featuring works by
CHRISTIAN FORMOSO
JEFF GUNDY
DIONNE CUSTER EDWARDS
TRAVIS McCLERKING
AMELIA GRAMLING
TERRY HERMSEN
HANNAH STEPHENSON

GREEN FISH PRESS

ISBN: 979-8-218-08377-9

Text and cover design by Josh Brandon
Original cover photo by elCarito
Printed and bound in the United States by Lightning Source
Type set in the Minion Pro, Filosofia, and Gioviale famies in Adobe InDesign

"We will not find the depth of these waters and their metaphors as long as we do not coin a more vast, luminous and inclusive memory, to open ourselves to a plural consciousness of our stories."

CONTENTS

Hannah Stephenson (Columbus, OH)

PREFACE
Jim Bates, director of Early Interval

    The 15th century in Europe saw a great awakening of sorts, a burgeoning curiosity and an interest in intellectual matters. This Renaissance of learning and the subsequent flourishing of the arts began in northern Italy and spread across Europe. Concurrent to these developments and a further outgrowth of the "curiosity" was the Age of Discovery. Spain and Portugal began to explore the seas beyond the Mediterranean region in the 15th century, resulting in trade routes to India, the colonization of the Americas and discoveries along the West Coast of Africa which brought a greater understanding of the world in its entirety. Soon the Dutch, English and French would join in the seafaring discoveries.

    But there would be revealed many downsides to the wonders of exploration. Trade routes were established that produced an exchange of goods—goods that included the transfer of animals, plants, insects, humans (often in the form of slaves) and communicable diseases. These trade routes made possible the quick and fluid movement of these goods and people around our globe. The great curiosity that brought about the Age of Discovery put into motion forces that would lead to conquest, greed and other unintended consequences. Consequences that would not fully reveal themselves for 500 years.

    And now, 500 years later we are in the midst of a Tempest, faced with the Age of Discovery end game. An end game that has caused the depletion of resources, the plundering of our oceans, the pollution of the planet and an ever-escalating climate disaster without clear and agreeable solutions.

    During the Renaissance the same wealth that financed risky explorations also fueled a desire for great works of art that reflected the era in abundant ways. In music, the sonic arts filled great cathedrals for the glory of God, and at court, musicians were deployed to entertain and demonstrate the wealth and taste of the affluent. This music, in all its emotive possibility, reflected the simplicity of daily life, the beauty and variety of nature, the earthly desires of mankind and even sometimes pushed past the earthly bonds to express the profound.

    This project seeks to bring together contemporary ideas and viewpoints expressed in word and verse with music composed during a more innocent time. Here is both the starting point and the end game. Perhaps by holding the two side by side in counterpoint, we can begin to fashion a pathway toward a solution, or at least consider how change can and must happen in this moment.

INTRODUCTION: WHEN TWO AGES MEET
Terry Hermsen, Editor

When E.M. Forster coined the phrase, "Only connect," he named something that we as artists, poets, musicians—and indeed all of us—are largely about. New thought happens when we place two things side by side… and see what results emerge. This goes deep into the heart of language. Place "astro" for stars beside "naut" for sea (or sailing) and we get "astronaut." Place "pan" for "all" beside "demon" for horror and we get "pandemonium." Long ago, someone in Anglo-Saxon times placed the world "clüd" (Old English for "rocky mass or hill") upon the creatures floating in the sky that became known as "clouds".

But here in a time of mass extinction of species and catastrophic disruption of the weather patterns that have sustained humanity for 10,000 years, we find ourselves in need of new metaphors—new ways to connect. At the close of 500 years of militarism and extraction, we still "aim" to meet our goals, we still speak of "expanding our reach" or being "blown out of the water." As if we still lived separately, in a single culture, making the earth ours, where "ignorant armies clash by night."

So maybe it's time for the music of the past to meet the poetry of the present so that we might "reach out" to know, rather than conquer, fostering and engaging our impulse to wonder about all that has happened in between, welcoming gardens and creatures, seasons and storms, even as we reconsider the "age of discovery" and face the tempest before us?

As I write this, one-third of Pakistan lies under water, much of that water coming from the melting glaciers high along its borders. Conversely, a deep drought stronger than any for 12,000 years has green the American plains—and a couple months ago, many towns in eastern Kentucky were flooded with rains 600 times stronger than they've ever received. A new tempest for sure, with new seas we must maneuver, seeking all the cooperation and ingenuity we can find. New skills of humanity and empathy. New ways of life, less destructive and consumptive. New ears and eyes for the nuances of creation. New words and voices for where we are now. As we used to say, all hands on deck… let us connect.

CHRISTIAN FORMOSO
Punta Arenas, Chile

is a Chilean poet. Among his verse collections are: *Puerto de hambre* (2005), *El cementerio más hermoso de Chile* (2008), *bellezamericana* (2014), and *WWM —Walt Whitman Mall—* (2020). Some of his poems have been translated to English, French, German and Greek and have appeared in anthologies, in Chile and abroad. Among other distinctions, he was awarded the National Council Prize for the Best Book Published in Chile for *El cementerio más hermoso de Chile* in 2009 and the Pablo Neruda Prize of the Pablo Neruda Foundation in 2010. He teaches Latin American literature at Universidad de Magallanes and holds an MFA from Vanderbilt and a PhD in Hispanic literature and languages from Stony Brook University.

His poems in this collection are all from *el cementerio más hermoso de Chile* (first published in Chile by Editorial Cuarto Proprio (2008). These translations are by Terry Hermsen, Sydney Tammarine and Andrea Pac. Previous versions appeared in *The Most Beautiful Cemetery in Chile* (Green Fish Press, 2015).

†

Beneath the blank page

Everything and all you can do is to say quiet, someone is prowling, the agitation of a single horseshoe, a furled mast above the speaking of a throat. Everything and all you can find is the head of an old epitaph carved into the white stem of a word. Beneath the page you see a ship and a shipwreck. You are the ship and the shipwreck.

Al fondo de la página blanca

Todo y lo menos posible es decir quieto, alguien ronda, el agitado tumulto de una sola herradura, un palo cerrado sobre el decir de una garganta. Todo y lo menos es hallar la cabeza de un viejo epitafio tallada en el tronco blanco de una palabra. Al fondo de la página ves un barco y un naufragio. Eres el barco y el naufragio.

THE DEPTHS OF THE SEA

1

The depths of the sea is not the depths of a rose, the depths of growing silence: the perpetual rose does not shed its glances before the waters; the depth of the rose is not the depths of the sea, but a shadow withers to lay down its seed, and in the imprint of its heel her measure of greed, and a tremor equates their countenances, when the rose returns to the depth of its stem, and the wave returns to the depths of the sea.

2

The depths of the salty glance of the seas, the depths of the thorn of the rose in its glances, the eyelash of the sea that the shipwrecked seize, the depths of the sea where glances open, the eyelash on the cheek where a letter hovers, the letter of the shipwreck lost in the mail, the envelope of bones dropped in the depths of the sea.

EL FONDO DE LA MAR

1

El fondo de la mar no es el fondo de una rosa, el fondo del silencio creciente: la rosa perpetua no deshoja su mirada ante las aguas; el fondo de la rosa no es el fondo de la mar, pero se marchita una sombra para llevar su semilla, y en su talón se encierra su codicia jalonada, y un temblor iguala sus señales, cuando la rosa vuelve al fondo de la rama, y la ola vuelve al fondo de la mar.

2

El fondo de la mirada salada de los mares, el fondo de la espina de la rosa en las miradas, la pestaña de la mar donde se aferran los náufragos, el fondo de la mar donde se abren las miradas, la pestaña en la mejilla de la que cuelga una carta, la carta de naufragio extraviada en el correo, el sobre con huesos olvidado al fondo de la mar.

from THE TEAR OF KOOCH WHICH CREATED THE MOST BEAUTIFUL CEMETERY IN CHILE

> *From the beginning of everything, Kooch was surrounded by shadows*
> *This saddened him so much that he began to cry*
> *So many were his tears that they formed the sea, where*
> *life began to take shape the life that would populate the world.*
> —LIFE AND LEGENDS OF THE TEHUELCHES
> MARIO ECHEVERRIA B.

I tell you that I love you even though I can only seen you in the inventory
of the dead, even though your hand does not reach beyond
your shattered love. Yesterday I excised your sight from a riverbed
of fire, where nothing arose but darkness before my
eyes. Before you I did not know the kiss of distance
nor the distance I now reside in, your time immemorial.
Yesterday is what time sowed over me before you
appeared, I was alone dressed in darkness from the
beginning, the empty pages over my face on
the screen, but your happiness tormented me, crowning the sea
as it formed, a white sea that was neither sea nor white
merely a being totally emptied of feeling, seeming like nothing, text
messages in unfamiliar jargon, other languages of vacancy
below a vacancy of form. Everything saddened me
in such a way that I began to cry, my tears for you
were deep and endless, and my tears were
enough to form the sea, and the sea aroused
my desire, and with my desire the throb of life. Because of my
tears you were born, just as I know you
cry for you and made you with my tears and in the models of you
I was populating all possible worlds, all
times were possible for discovering
your eyes, such as I saw them fixed in a coffin of my
shadow, but your eyes were lost in the sea
and to see them incarnated in me, I released the sigh of the wind
that shook the darkness, and I saw the light assisting your birth, I assembled
one by one the bones for you, the bright sheet of day
I laid over you, the flames of the flowers to place
the throb in your chest, with the garland of summer to adorn
your waist, for your neck I plucked the stem
of high noon, your hands were brought from the paradise
of doves. Your voice made mine tremble
like a river, all then from the depths of the great depths
of what is neither white nor sea with moans and heat

the white borders and hot center of fire, and from the center
of the flame the tide of the years, and of the years its glow
for you. […]

Juan Diaz del Valle, sailor, native of Comillas

I was once a strong man, not this vessel undermined by hunger and destiny. I dreamed of a mansion of clear water with its allotment of light and shadow. I nourished the horse of my childhood who galloped through every league, and every wave dragged through my dissolution, at the same pace as my steadiness, in a light of miraculous fires, of masts aflame, of sea-weed bound words that guided my prow toward the wave, my head toward the depths of the interior hold, my mouth toward a tiny star in an anchored sail –to the end– of a shipwreck.

Once I was a strong man. With my extended staff I pierced through the night and anchored my song in the hearts of certain daughters, certain waves of the wide unknown, who with kisses dreamed of breaking the rocks, with the words adrift before the shipwreck was over. Then the summer dried my gaze, and the hunger devoured so many times all my intentions. And it assaulted me, the clamor of the squall, the rage of a god who extended me an underwater hand. I sobbed for so many nights, heart wounded by the wind, leaving a slipstream of blood over the map of my journeys.

If once I was a strong man, what shall I do now scattered in the ash? Whose voice turned my dream to ash? And why a tablet instead of my eyes

Juan Díaz del Valle, marinero, natural de Comillas

Yo fui alguna vez un hombre fuerte, no esta nave minada por el hambre y el destino. Yo soñé la mansión del agua clara con ración de luz y de penumbra. Yo alimenté mi caballo de niño que galopaba en cada legua, y cada ola arrastró mis destrozos a razón de mi paciencia, a la luz de fuegos milagrosos, de mástiles encendidos, de palabras de sargazo que guiaron mi nariz hacia la ola, mi cabeza hacia lo hondo de *bodegas interiores,* mi boca hacia una estrella diminuta en la vela anclada –al fin– de un naufragio.

Yo alguna vez fui un hombre fuerte. Con mi bastón extendido atravesé la noche y anclé mi canción en lo hondo de unas hi-jas, unas olas del todo desconocidas, que soñaban con romper a besos las rocas, con la palabra a la deriva ante el naufragio consumado. Después el estío secó mi mirada, y el hambre devoró tantas veces mi designio. Y me asaltó el clamor de la borrasca, la cólera de un dios que me tendía su mano submarina. Sollocé tantas noches, herido el corazón por el viento, dejando una estela de sangre sobre el mapa de mis derrotas.

Si alguna vez fui un hombre fuerte, qué hago ahora repartido en la ceniza? de quién la voz que hizo ceniza mi sueño? por qué una tabla en lugar de mis ojos?

Testimony of the indian who refuses to say his name

The unknown Indian
arrived from the mists of a nebulous history
and geography. He lies here covered with
the love of the true Chilean spirit
"eternally"
—Epitaph for the statue of the unknown indian
the cemetery of punta arenas

Call me whatever you want because it is not me you name, nor am I the one for whom you light these candles, nor the one you have entombed among the dead. I am not the one who will give them *your spoonful of hope, your cup of love, your zest of patience*, it is not to me you carry these tablets and plaques, nor to me you request these favors that I do not want to give. I know there is a clothesline in each patio and from there they hang the tombs you wash once a week. In the kitchen you peel vegetables, make soup from bones, and lay down –once a week– over a soft corpse, rising up pale and sunbathe below the lampposts. There is a line in each room of the house and from there you hang the tombs that you wash once a week. In your inboxes you receive messages from Mexico, favor chains, appeals which you sign and send for the boy with leukemia who for each one hundred messages receives a dollar. It is not for me you pledge to leave this house, nor am I the one who asks life from a dead person I never knew. There is a clothesline in each bathroom in every house, and from this you hang the tombs you wash once a week. While you wait for them to dry, your wives light candles, pray, open and close the curtains, on Sundays rise very late and buy *El Magallenes*. Occasionally, you visit the cemetery, talk about the last time you saw your grandparents, of the homemade breads the elders used to make, the curanto and various sayings that remain in your ears. A cat up in a tree surprises you, a dog barks at you, an airplane passes over and you believe it is God.

TESTIMONIO DEL INDIO QUE REHÚSA DECIR SU NOMBRE

Llámenme como quieran pues no es a mí a quien llaman, ni a quien prenden velas, ni a quien tienen rodeado de muertos. No soy yo quien va a darles su *cucharada de esperanza, su taza de amor, su ralladura de paciencia*, no es a mí a quien llevan tablas y placas, ni a quien agradecen favores que no detengo. Sé que hay un cordel de ropa en cada patio y que de allí cuel-gan las tumbas que lavan una vez a la semana. En la cocina pelan verduras, hacen sopa de huesos, se acuestan –una vez a la semana– sobre un cadáver blando, se levantan blancos y se solean bajo los palos de luz. Hay un cordel en cada pieza de la casa, y de allí cuelgan las tumbas que lavan una vez a la semana. En sus casillas reciben mensajes de México, cadenas de favores, correos que firman y envían por el niño leucémico que cada cien mensajes recibe un dólar. No es por mí por quien votan para dejar esta casa, ni soy quien pide la vida a un muerto que no conoce. Hay un cordel en cada baño de cada casa, y de allí cuelgan las tumbas que lavan una vez a la sema-na. Mientras esperan que sequen, las esposas encienden velas, rezan y abren y cierran las cortinas, los domingos se levantan muy tarde y compran *El Magallanes*. De vez en cuando visitan el cementerio, hablan del día que vieron por última vez a sus abuelos, de los panes amasados que los viejos solían hacer, de los curantos y algunas frases que se quedaron en sus oídos. Un gato sobre un árbol los sorprende, un perro les ladra, pasa un avión y creen que es Dios.

OPEN PRAIRIE GRAVE

Across the dry yellow blades the beam from the ghostly lighthouse
has been shut off, and the hairline pulled back
to reveal its inconclusive synchronicity, the wing of an estancia
disappearing below the shouting of the transparent laborers,
their work in the open air of the pasture impassioned
with solitude. The ships that continue slowly falling
from the bottom of a goblet encrusted and salty, herds of horses
succeeded by wagons of drought, barbed wire
stretched out with its slow seeds dripping from the depths
of earth, a grieving chirp in poor imitation
of the old fires. Over
the dry blades flags open in bloom
emaciated yet still burning
beneath the pious prevarication of the snow, beneath the regal piety
of the resurgent frost, emptied of significance. Seeming to
stride away the remaining walls rise like the steps
of sleepwalkers, under the hair
of an infinity that limits
with the stumbling and stuttering tumbling
from the mouth, from the turbulent distance, like a pathway
without branches, emptiness before the eyebrows that lay out a yellow hue
extended evenly over a burning canvas, and over this
there are black bulls and interminable herds of sheered
sheep, skeleton dogs, and dead shepherds
that tame the yellow horse they mount
in the distance, and the black horse
that, escaping, rides off through the dry arroyo
in summer, the lagoon that in spring bears an oasis
for the birds, the flamingo that opens the yellow
arena of the year. Like a slippery fish it all
leaves nothing but a vagueness and the bleeding
of these revelations, the silent articulation of the pieces
of a cog that scatter between languages and thorny
names at the edge of a road bunched up
with tar, with the deceptive sensation of bringing life back
at the closing curve of death. In front of *El Cerro del
Cazador*, a cemetery that warns of what's to come: a pair
of crosses without names over the yellow flicker of a distant
lighthouse, both of the day and of the mountain, in the middle
of a flat land without any shores. And waves of pastures restless
in the wind. No ship adrift, not a single man
falling through water, merely to the earth. A poem without commas,
with rhymes, left only partially complete.

TUMBA PAMPA ABIERTA

Sobre la seca sobra amarilla se ha apagado la luz de un
faro perdido, y la partidura del cabello se ha revelado
para abrir su sincronía inconclusa, el alero de una estancia
desaparecida bajo los gritos de jornales transparentes
la faena descubierta sobre el pastizal inflamado de
quietud. Los barcos que continúan cayendo desde
el fondo de una copa enquistada y salobre, las tropillas
seguidas por el camión de la sequía, los alambres de púa
tendidos con sus semillas lentas entrando desde el fondo
de la tierra, un piar acongojado de viejos incendios
repetidos en versiones menos acabadas. Sobre
la sobra seca se abre una floración reproducida
con banderas enjutas que aún arden
bajo la mentira piadosa de la nieve, bajo lo real piadoso
de la escarcha establecida, vaciada de significado. Zancadas
parecen esas sobras que suben sobre el desvelo
lanzado, bajo la cabellera de un infinito que limita
con el tropiezo y el tartamudeo, que escapa
de la boca, de la distancia agitada, como un paseo sin
ramas, vacío frente a las cejas que coronan un amarillo
que parejo se extiende sobre un lienzo quemado, y sobre eso
hay toros negros y rebaños interminables de ovejas
esquiladas, y perros esqueletos y ovejeros muertos
que amansan el caballo amarillo
que montan a la distancia, y el caballo negro
que se les va como pagado por el arroyo seco
en verano, la laguna que en primavera es un oasis
para los pájaros, el flamenco que hace del amarillo
parte de su año. De todo como de un pez escurridizo
no hay más que la imprecisión y la sangría de estas
revelaciones, la callada articulación de las piezas
de engranaje que se esparcen entre lenguas y nombres
espinosos, a la orilla de un camino atado
al alquitrán, y la *engañosa* sensación de reverdecimiento
al final de la curva de la muerte. Frente al Cerro del
Cazador, un cementerio avisa lo que sigue: un par
de cruces sin nombre sobre el piar amarillo de un faro
distante tanto del día como de la montaña, en medio
de una pampa sin orillas. Y olas de pasto movidas
por el viento. Barco ninguno a la deriva, hombre
ninguno cayendo al agua, sino a la tierra. Poema
sin comas, con rima, a medio terminar.

A young boy begs to find *la esperanza*

Behind the wall of the church
I painted it the boat that I ask for
for Christmas, I ask for one hundred boats
entering the Port before
I grow up I want
also one hundred toy boats
and a tree full
of tickles, of terror.
But mostly the boats and no more
crying for my brother, nor word
of my mother, but boats
that one boat, please.
I promise you, I'll
behave, I want
the boats
to carry me to the sun.
Many more boats I want
one hundred more boats, better still
let it be a thousand.

Un niño pide encontrar la esperanza

Detrás de la pared de la iglesia
yo pinté el ese barco que yo pido
para Navidad, yo pido cien barcos
entrando en el Puerto antes
que yo sea grande quiero
y también cien barcos de juguete
y un árbol lleno
de cosquillas, de terror.
Pero mejor los barcos y no
más lágrima para mi hermano, ni palabra
de mi madre, sino barcos
ese barco uno, por favor
te prometo, portarme
bien yo quiero
que los barcos
me lleven hasta el sol.
Muchos más barcos quiero
cien más barcos, mejor
que sean mil.

WRITTEN A MILLION YEARS AGO

First came looking in the mirror of the waters, although before
the looking was the hearing of one's name in whatever place
we heard it. Only before that, perhaps, it was a madness, the stone
attached to the bottom of the stream and loosened in tiny
movements. When this stone arrives at the shore
then begins the naming. To know what we call it
takes another hundred thousand years, and equally tons of
water, and equally kilometers of wind to release it to nothing among
other pebbles. By the time the stone has crossed over
to its vegetal beginnings, we start hearing what
we're hearing, though it must first take root and
open to the warmth of movement. Only then do we begin
to call, although at first –so to speak– we are alone
and surrounded by darkness, it is our tears that birth
the waters where later we will see ourselves, and the sigh
that follows the tears that gives origin to the wind that will arrive
to undo the stone. Into these waters goes that which
we hear, we leave from them to spill ourselves onto the shore
and then find a way to mend these same waters
again. What we hear withdraws and returns
with waves the color of blood from the sea of blood. With
each wave it sheds its sound. To create this sound takes us
as many years as it takes the stone to reach the depths
of our blood. From there the rest dissolves like a dream.
The first dream –as already said– was named Kooch, and was able to
dream without anyone having opened the secrets
of its thickets we push through
now. Only no one noticed that Kooch would arrive
again, and stay in the shadows waiting for a ship
that would birth once again his same body and the same body
we push through now. What we name
stumbles near to this repeated stigma. Enclosed,
we said, surrounded by water, we listen to hear pieces
of what we heard. What we call opened first
in its anguish, then in its reiteration, and then it was
just a part of the scheme, but what we say
has a density that overcomes us if we look behind.
Facing the screen, now we say surf. We call
and listen at the same time and there is nothing but a reiteration
of what we hear. It would all be the same as saying we are
in a ship's cabin surrounded by light and then
we begin to cry. The keys rhyme against the solitude

of this cabin and make room so we can hear
the names we have called. It's all an example and a way
of speaking. The reiteration
continues if we realize that we repeat the same old sailing
songs, and the repeated face on the screen
is equally repeated just like the face
over the water. All of these convergences are but pieces
of that which we hear, and what still rhymes
with the keys is part of what we called after
the tears. Before the sea. And before returning to listen.

Escrito hace un millón de años

Primero fue mirarse en el espejo de las aguas, aunque antes
de mirarse fue oír el nombre de uno en el lugar donde
lo oímos. Sólo que antes, tal vez, estaba el desvarío, la piedra
que sujeta al fondo del arroyo se libera en pequeños
movimientos. Cuando esa piedra llega a la orilla
entonces comienza lo que llamamos. Saber qué llamamos
toma otros cientos de miles de años, y otras toneladas
de agua, y otros kilómetros de viento para deshacerla
entre otras piedrecillas. Para cuando la piedra ha entrado
en su parto vegetal, podemos empezar a oír aquello
que escuchamos, aunque antes deba enraizarse y llegar
a abrirse al tibio movimiento. Sólo después empezamos
a llamar, y aunque primero –es un decir– estamos solos
y rodeados de tinieblas, es nuestro llanto del que nacen
las aguas donde después nos miraremos, y el suspiro
que sigue al llanto, lo que da origen al viento que llegará
a deshacer esa piedra. En esas aguas va lo que
escuchamos, salimos de ellas para volcarnos a la orilla
y luego buscar la forma de remontar las mismas aguas
nuevamente. Lo que escuchamos se repliega y vuelve
con olas del color de la sangre de la mar de la sangre. Con
cada ola se deshoja su sonido. Componer el sonido entero
 nos lleva tantos años como le lleva a la piedra llegar al fondo
de nuestra sangre. De ahí el resto se desata como en un sueño.
El primer sueño –ya se dijo– se llamó Kooch, y fue capaz
de soñar sin que nadie hubiese abierto los secretos
de la espesura por donde ahora abrimos nuestro
paso. Pero nadie reparó que Kooch vendría luego
también solo, y quedaría en las tinieblas esperando un barco
que daría a luz nuevamente su mismo cuerpo y el mismo cuerpo
por donde ahora abrimos nuestros pasos. Lo que llamamos
se acerca a ese estigma repetido. Encerrado
decíamos, rodeados de agua, escuchamos a pedazos
lo que escuchamos. Lo que llamamos se ha abierto primero
en su angustia, luego en su reiteración, y nosotros después
sólo una parte del esquema, pues lo que decimos
tiene una densidad que nos supera si miramos hacia atrás.
Frente a la pantalla, ahora decimos navegar. Llamamos
y escuchamos al mismo tiempo y no es sino reiteración
de lo que escuchamos. Sería lo mismo decir que estamos
en la cabina rodeados de luz y que entonces
empezamos a llorar. Las teclas riman contra la soledad

de esa cabina y hacen espacio para dejar oír
que llamamos. Es un ejemplo y un decir. La reiteración
sigue si caemos en cuenta que repetimos la cantinela
del navegar, y que el rostro repetido en la pantalla
está igualmente repetido y del mismo modo que el rostro
sobre el agua. Todas esas constataciones no son sino
pedazos de lo que oímos, y lo que sigue rimado
con sus teclas es parte de lo que llamamos después
del llanto. Antes de la mar. Y antes de volver a escuchar.

JEFF GUNDY
Bluffton, Ohio

is Distinguished Poet in Residence at Bluffton University. His thirteen books include *Wind Farm: Landscape with Stories and Towers,* an exploration of the Illinois landscape, history, and memoir in lyric essays and photographs, recently published by Dos Madres Press. Other recent books include *Without a Plea* and *Abandoned Homeland* (Bottom Dog Press) and *Songs from an Empty Cage: Poetry, Mystery, Anabaptism, and Peace* (criticism). His poems and essays appear in *Georgia Review, The Sun, Kenyon Review, Forklift, Ohio, Christian Century, Image, Cincinnati Review, Terrain,* and other journals. He held a Fulbright lectureship at the University of Salzburg in 2008 and was named Ohio Poet of the Year in 2015 for *Somewhere Near Defiance.*

DEERFLY

When I was a red-winged blackbird I knew every post and stump, I could tell exactly when it was time to fly.

When I was a waterlily I gave all my best leaves to the pond, and my best blossoms too.

When I was a cattail I knew my friends and my numerous enemies by their scent and their shape and the size of their stems.

When I was the multiflora rose I found many cozy spots, I was thorny but hip, I was nicer to the bluebirds than to the crows.

When I was the duckweed I stuck to any bird I could, half the time I didn't even bother with the flowers, just split whenever I got the chance.

When I was the pond I rested for weeks on end, let the wind and the sun do all the work, said *whatever* all the time.

When I was the sun I had many urgent and utopian ideas, I changed millions of tons of this into that, I didn't care who watched or burned themselves blind trying.

When I was the path everybody thought they used me, but they all went exactly where I wanted them to go.

When I was Jeff I walked some paths, sat beside ponds, listened to songs I couldn't name. During the eclipse I looked straight at the sun for an instant and afterwards I could still see, though never as clear nor as far as I dreamed.

When I was a deerfly I zoomed around everybody's head, as if I could persuade them my troubles were their own.

Somewhere near defiance

It's late but everything comes next.
　　　　　—Naomi Shihab Nye, "Jerusalem"

1.
I live near Defiance, a white name pressed on an old place.
Mad Anthony Wayne's soldiers broke down the orchards

when the battle was theirs, and built a fort
where the Auglaize and Maumee Rivers meet.

Water will answer anything, the moon, the wind,
the mud. The rivers mingle and move on.

2.
Once I drove my little car right into the heart of the empire,
huddled with my friends to plot and complain. All over town

the poets and other malcontents were hiding in the open,
vowing to split the rocks and terrify the despots.

In the coffeehouse we tallied our losses and wondered how
to subvert the lyric *I* until the hot waitress grabbed the mike

to say that racism wasn't over yet. We clapped for her,
then wandered toward the Capitol, launched some ragged

words to each other and the wind. All right, you can
have *shock,* we told the adversary, but *awe* belongs to us.

3.
Walt Whitman thought his poems might stop the war.
When they did not he moved to Washington, took a day job

so he could go to the field hospitals, read to the wounded,
write letters for men with no arms or eyes. *I have been hurt*

but am mending well. Do not weep, I will find you one day.
I walked around for days, found no field hospitals,

lots of monuments. I passed the suited and booted,
shaggy and lame, proud and weary, and it seemed

that each of us carried a wound we were trying to hide.

4.
Meanwhile the drone pilots turn their Hellfires loose
from dark rooms in the suburbs, buy a 6-pack on the way home.

1200 veterans of the last good war die each day,
and the stools at the VFW stand like puzzled mushrooms.

5.
These days I wake up grateful that my heavy dreams are gone.
I snag the zipper of my coat, pull it free, and walk off

puzzling over slides and words and stratagems. Then I step
into a room and see a row of faces, hopeful and new

as yellow apples hanging in the orchards of Defiance.

6.
The morning came brilliant to my quiet town,
sun in the junipers, a robin on the wire.

Nothing that I do matters to the earth or the sky.

But I've stalled around too long—it's time for declarations,
time for floods. Time to put down the *Toledo Blade*

and take a very long walk. Time to say peace on terror,
peace on drugs, peace on Defiance.

Peace on Mad Anthony and his soldiers—gone so quiet now—
and the warriors they fought, and the fruit trees they tore.

The Auglaize and the Maumee join and drift on,
exchanging sticks and soil and bits of news.

We are in the earth already, and the earth in us.

Even from Defiance, nothing's more than half a world away.

ADDITIONAL ASSERTIONS ON SOUL

Only moving does it have a soul.
—PABLO NERUDA, "ODE TO BICYCLES"

1. All stones, even those from the moon, must share a single soul.

2. Dragonflies each have the soul of another, and spend their lives chasing their own.

3. Barns have souls until the main timber breaks.

4. Birds have souls only when singing, flying, or at rest.

5. Butterflies are so light because they abandon their souls at birth.

6. Automobiles have souls made of grease and fire, just like us.

7. The heron's soul is all bone and feathers, an excellent mother despite its lack of hands and breasts.

8. The tiger lily's flower is tender and sweet on the tongue, and its soul likewise.

9. We believe the earth has a soul, but nobody has ever gotten its attention.

10. The many tiny souls of the grass were at perfect ease until Whitman began to ask questions.

11. The air is one wild soul looking blindly for the lost one.

12. And the water, oh it carries many souls, but keeps none for itself.

Contemplation with ledges and moon

What do the hollows in the stone promise?
Where the scratched names stop, the rock mutters

what it meant all along. Here, the grizzled red maple.
There, yellow beech clenched hard to the cliff side,

a tulip tree smooth forty feet up. Edges blur
in the half-light, and the swallows work higher

and higher, and the bats revel, stretching
their thin webs around what they need.

The mind is a rattly gourd, the ego, a black marble.
The soul is very light and large, a cloud of leaves

that froth and fade into the wood thrush's cry.
There is no soul without the shy veery,

the whiny bugs hunting our heat, the gravel
working its way out from sandstone.

The soul is not a language or a cat or a catapult.
It is a net without mesh, a sail knuckling and filling

among fireflies and gauzy leaves, flowing into
every valley, filling every breath and stone, spinning,

keening, rising, dusty heartwood, silken fog.
The broken path through trees made us stumble,

but we found the wide meadow at last
where the great golden moon lifted up

from the well of her sleep and sent down
more borrowed light than we needed

as we cried out and whispered on our way.

AMBITIONS

These are woods that forgive everything but forget nothing.
— TOMAS TRANSTRÖMER

To be a forest dense and green enough to hide a million creatures

To be the vine grown right to the top of the tallest tree

To be the man whose job is to save the tree by sawing through the vine three feet up

To be the bench waiting just when a man needs a rest

To be the sign that answers the question the man hasn't asked yet

To carry back the names: willow, buttonbush, boxelder maple, spatterdock and fragrant waterlily

Water smartweed and the endangered wapato, midge and mayfly and whirligig beetle

Green darner dragonfly, vivid dancer damselfly

And always the large dim roar of many narrow waves hurrying in

To stand at the edge until one laps at my shoes

To touch the water and think *I could swim*

To cross back over the barrier beach, the only human sound my footsteps

Many insects, a high gentle wind stirring everything

Countless volunteers, the last sign remembers

To volunteer at last

THE GOD OF DIRT

came up to me & scowled
and asked me what we'd done
with the treasure. Sorry,
I said, I can't even
tell you where it went,
Lake Erie, the St. Lawrence,
we barely noticed.

Well then, said the god
of dirt, *taste & see*
& there she was,
unknown & yet
I knew her,
had seen her
in some hollow of the mind,
flitting & calling,
& not for me,
not to me.

Listen said the god
of dirt & she sang
liquid & lovely
tangled up my body
& mind in blue
and gold and green
thickets of song.

Then she whispered
something soft to me
& spun herself away,
whispered to me
something soft
that I will not say.

THE WIND FARMER RELEASES THE WIND

The strange notion of rûaḥ in the Hebrew Scriptures shatters taxonomies, leaving us to ask mistakenly, "Is rûaḥ wind? Breath? Spirit? Or spirit?" In particular, rûaḥ causes tidy dichotomies to splinter, neat categories to fragment.
    —JACK LEVISON, *A BOUNDLESS GOD*

There are no crosses on the wind farm. The turbines, with their three blades and the great arcs they make, refuse the stasis of upright and crossbeam, they brook no fixed readings. Bound as they are to their singular place they are also free, they spin, they make their rounds.

And wind is breath is spirit in Hebrew after all, the blades are tuned and turned to the wind, to the spirit, nothing men have ever made is so cleverly, closely tuned, so capable of drawing true power from what looks like nothing, what moves beyond chance or habit in its great whorls and streams.

What preacher in his oaken fort can hope to speak so craftily, so truly of the power, of the sizzle and shame, the buzz and hum and emptiness spinning in the heart of things. What nun or priest or worship singer could chant or sing so precisely so well of the secret messenger,

the vast and complicated wind, the wind without border or end, the wind that is ghost and spirit, the inbreath and outbreath of the being more real and tenuous than dark matter, than strings or quarks or whatever particles, spins, sparkling bits of almost nothing make up the heart of the real,

the spirit, the wind, the breath, and yes, what can sing like the long blunt blades of the wind machine, the blades that cut nothing but the wind and know the wind flows back together, always, smoother than any water.

DIONNE CUSTER EDWARDS
Columbus, Ohio

is a writer, educator, and director of Learning & Public Practice at the Wexner Center for the Arts. She also founded the award-winning art and writing program *Pages*. Dionne has published critical and literary writing, internationally and nationally in *Sanat Dünyamiz* ("Our Art World"), Turkey; *Journal GEARTE*, Brazil; and in the University of Arizona's *Journal of Cultural Research in Art Education*.

Her literary work has appeared in *3Elements Review, Barren Magazine, Entropy Magazine, Flock, Gordon Square Review, Grist, Porter House Review, Storm Cellar, The Seventh Wave, Tahoma Literary Review,* and others. Dionne is co-editor of a book series, forthcoming, to be published by Ohio State University Press, *On Possibility: Social Change and the Arts + Humanities*. Dionne has an MA in arts education and creative writing, Antioch University and a BA in English, The Ohio State University.

American History Elevator Pitch

One day we will talk about ghosts.
Find a way to miracle.

Name a once-river a sober row,
Or hybrid sweet shiny lie with plastics,
long crawl down a halfway magic,
trouble.

For now, we call it home. This land
of fertile knot of self and star-like wounds.
A small debt of death and heat

in our throats. Swallow of hot iron cruel.
And in fairness, a curtain of kindness.

Notice the manner of kindness:
at dinner parties, on front porches,
across the street, around cubicle walls.
When we unearth this soil, we loosen
the soothe. Stumble on the silence.
I wait.
Give my American history elevator pitch:
A few strangers, heavy hands on land,

on people. A concoction of pecking orders,
feuds and sparks. They called it freedom.
Some sorted details, time, peril, left out.

This country spread its long thick spine
between the oceans,
Became a ribbon of glorious terrible deeds.
Born between the legs of heroes and thorns.
Bitter, sweet, rotten, wicked, free.

A place to lay the storm

Galveston, Texas, 1900

Before we named storms, it rained into the gulf until it hurt.
Toppled over salt cedars, past short roots in dunes.
Skin, timber, slate and debris, the bowels of a barrier broke open,
swallowed an island whole. The streets mud and color-filled.
Floods are casual strange betrayals, a furious cleansing,
a dispassionate and particular kind of purge.
When the body is no longer yours, death is a dwelling.
Drowned inside every sweat drunk curl along the hairline.
Under armpits, up to chin and shoulders, a wide-awake rising tide.
Water seeped down into cracks in the ground.
Amassed as heaping stream over a course of bones.
Branches and limbs suffered the same. A shred of living things
cracked by white sheets of rain, spit, and wind.
After tempest slowed, sea level rose like fear and vanishing.
Sudden jut of frantic and fend, a wet island sure with grief.

In sour waters, all high ground sinks in peril. Flood hushed
the coast. Full air stench of camphor and whiskey dulled the horror.

A small crawl of them left to raise the dead. Miles of drenched
ember, more than the ground or mouth could hold or tell.

When the body is no longer yours, death is a yard of voices.

Plastic in the Salt

Safe functions as folklore, ignores
a dark cylinder room. The equivalent

of five plastic grocery bags piled
inside of every foot of coastline

along the planet. A million particles
floating in brine end up gathered

in a dry process. Sharp crystals
extracted, lodged in the throat

and lungs of living things. A piece
of marine food chain, fresh, inedible.
I threw away the coarse white sea salt.
Recycled the cardboard container.

How do you cure single use plastics?
I kept the fine cut salt in the cabinet until
I could wrap my mind around a dilemma.
The alternative, season food with flecks

of drinking straws, cheap small toys,
sandwich bags, distilled like secrets.

Slow leak

We tell our stories by mouth
and by keeping. Things in a box

look precious. Abundant
looks free, formed in a communion

of spare. Notes looking for space,
for pieces of a revolution.

We invented ruin.
Something like slow decay
sprinkled over skin, food,

breathing, an unfinished work
of strangers who intervened.

Like a whip of sawdust,
body of water with a leak, we insist

on unraveling, growing like weeds
all over the place,

looking for edges to fill.
Some say,
we cannot avoid how hard
and long it rains, burns, or blows.

Others say,
nothing.

GESTURE TO HIGH WATER

How much storm can we stand? Watching
people suffer looks like a set of old ideas

stranded on a ledge. More rain, mud, rumors,
spread fast and falsely. A posture offering help.

A sad swim looking for flowers, for petals
in a flood. What are the holes in our knowing?

The exterior space, the rind, defined for us,
a quilted myth. After water spilling,
what will our grind and abstracts witness?
Human beings in a crux. We sit around a fable

with a valve leaking. Small gestures respond
to high water. The rooftop sits in the sky.

DES DAUGHTER

The first time I felt the stretch and well size
of a womb, my body, the shape of a small desire,

was a soft spot inside of you. Submerged
in fatigue and will, I must have heard you trying

to save me with suppository and quarrel. After
ample amounts of weeping for all the ones

before me, a chemical disrupting harmony meant
you could keep me inside you for a while longer.

But safety tastes different a generation later.
Pill and water in skin a bit more pinch and spiked

in a full-lunged life. I imagine you drawing
an origin with as many curled and wing sharp

lines as you could realize. A chemical shaped
like wish and stars negotiated labor and ends,

secretion of weeds in a field of flowering

needles and chance, desperate act of keeping.

TOXIC FREE

We root and raise our young in the failing.
We did not disturb the asbestos.
Pregnancy poses new choices.
The water, soil, air already altered. Somewhere
somebody chooses the opposite of collapse.
The babies smile. We hide our grief. Security
and freedom fall through the cracks.
The ozone crumbling. Sun shaped like trouble.
I do not remember my mom pregnant. Twice.
We did not filter the water then. I sat on ice
after my first two births. By the third,
I pressed the landlord to remedy the lead
paint. Before we bought the house, we lived in
what our money could buy. The toxic was free.

Hostile ground

We do not see neighboring as fatal.
Not everyone can move from hostile ground.
Fine mist of unpleasant, pollutant, poor
environmental condition. A dirty hand,
mold, arsenic, lead, a perpetual venom.
Who will live by a gutter on a trash hill?
Hazardous appears eager in a cradle.
Please do not walk barefoot on few choices.
The lead paint in the bathroom peeled
from the walls and ceiling. We stripped
that wet room down to the studs.
We did not want the babies
to put satin in their mouths.
In a city, waste wears on a lung, skin, tongue.
Trace amounts of refinery, landfill,
incinerator, erosion, brooding over a life.
Things we make get dumped somewhere,
on someone.

LAUREL ANDERSON
Delaware, Ohio

is a plant ecologist and holder of the Morris Family Professorship in Natural Sciences in the Department of Botany and Microbiology at Ohio Wesleyan University. She is also president of the board of directors for the Ecological Research as Education Network (EREN). Anderson's research and teaching interests include temperate forest ecology, invasive plants, global environmental change, environmental issues in food production, and developing collaborative ecological projects across small colleges. She leads travel courses on global change in Brazil, Utah and Alaska. In 2015, she was recognized as the Ohio Professor of the Year by the Carnegie Foundation for the Advancement of Teaching and the Council for Advancement and Support of Education. Laurel is also a poet. Her poetry has appeared or is forthcoming in *Terrain.org* (semi-finalist in the 12th annual poetry contest), *Radar Poetry, EcoTheo Review, Split Rock Review* and elsewhere. Laurel teaches science at Ohio Wesleyan University and lives with her family in central Ohio, USA.

ABOVE THE RIVER

Two flowering dogwoods
hang into space, each
clutching the cliff
with one wooden fist
while their blossoms
hover over dark water
like swarms of white bees.
Canada geese bugle upstream
and the sun continues
the work of closing up.
At the right moment, the river
becomes a trail of pulsing light
weaving between walls
of crumbling shale
and the boy who skips stones
under falling petals
sees his stone shrug off heaviness
and leap across the last
breath of day spreading
like gold silk
on the water's lap.

WILLOW

There was a field deep in urban nowhere
with an old willow in the center.
My friend and I would sneak
through a gap in the chain-link fence
and sit for hours beneath the tree, its
trailing ropes of leaves enclosing us
in a domed chamber like a great, green bell.
Sunflecks speckled our laps as we wove
dandelion crowns with our small hands
and small alliances with our small tongues.
Now, I see two young girls, easy prey
in their pretend palace. I wonder when
I learned to feel alone and far from help
in the company of tree, flower, grass, sky.

#INSECTAPOCALYPSE. A THREAD.

In a world where cognition is currency,
we are the underclass. Forebrain, midbrain, hindbrain
in miniature, just enough to keep the lights on.

Yet, we know beauty. Green glimmer-gloss of beetles,
glitterpane wings and faceted eyes,
tiny eggs afloat in jeweled froth stitched to grass.

We know sickness. We bring nightmares
of fever and rash, ache in the bone,
twist of the botfly beneath the taut skin.

We know family. In a palace of paper and wax,
her half sisters hum as they circle the queen, feeding her,
bathing her, tending her brood in their hexagon cradles.

We know vengeance. The hornet that enters the hive
as a hunter is surrounded, restrained, and roasted alive
in the heat of one thousand vibrating wings.

We know love. We fly caresses of pollen
from flower to flower so apples will weigh down
branches in autumn and almonds will fill with sweet oil.

We care for the dead. When a creature with fur
or feathers lays itself down the last time, we unravel
the threads of the body and sing them back into atoms.

We were a multitude. Our abundance powered
the flitter of bats, thrum of the bullfrog,
skitter of lizards through mazes of stone.

We die now as dust in mouths of dry rivers.
We crisp in the noon of a day that melts tar.
We emerge too early and starve without blossoms.

We explode into splats on the windshield.
We ash on a million hot lightbulbs.
We die twitching and slow in pesticide fogs that twist through green blades of corn.

We know that you do not mourn us.
You will.

Climate change, ohio

Day blazes toward golden honey noon.
Purple coneflowers stand stiff
stare at the sun
waiting for absent bees.

The river gorged last night
on 4 inches of dark rain
and now remembers ocean
as it rises and spreads silver
into the woods along each shore.

Trees hike their green skirts high
as they begin to wade the cornfields.

MARCHING ORDERS

Thick quilt of July
smothers the meadow.
Even the cottonwood
lacks strength to tremor.
The wild roses exploded early,
now droop, fade, crisp.
Heat musters its forces
joule by joule under carbon's
marching orders. The woods
are still cool but the trees
read portents in sun flecks,
foretell the coal-fired
ovens of August, brace
for parch and cull.
In lurid strobes of midnight
lightning, Ohio sleeps
through thunder's drum
as Arkansas trudges north.

Prayer of the frequent flyer

O Lord
I am aloft in a mighty silver machine that flings aside angels
as it burns and steams and roars
toward the western edge of North America.

The inflight movie flickers from seatback to seatback
like lightning leaps in white thunderheads
and whispers a story of war
through our headphones.

29,000 feet below,
green discs of irrigated cropland
polka-dot dry prairie.
Water coaxed from stone capillaries
climbs ladders of xylem up and up
to burst from the many-lipped leaves of corn
and join us here in the air.

Millions of people blown to ashes.
Millions of people fed by deep waters.
Millions of us each day
gliding on carbon's hot breath, laughing
at the authority of gravity.

Is it any wonder
I cry out to you
and ask that you
hold this plane
and all of us
in your hand?

MIDNIGHT, AIRPORT PARKING LOT

Asphalt cools, congeals, a black mask
across Earth's face.

Streetlights look down, illuminate
white herringbone lines

where cars sleep in straight rows
like people who wait.

Fireflies blink in the hush of grass
along runways, flash

ancient codes of longing, semaphore
guiding us back from the sky.

City park, quarantine

Soccer field grass clipped
like shorn heads of the fevered
back in the day, yet
some contagion I applaud.
Lemon light, flood the pitch,
dandelions the mower missed,
lift your backlit silver spun sugar tops,
dissolve into fluffy driftseed
unsnapping from succulent
green pedestals, seek
a place to bite and suckle soil,
explode into leaf, gold bloom, repeat.

TRAVIS McCLERKING
Columbus, Ohio

is a Sophomore at Ohio State University, Marion majoring in English. He has been published in *Hooligan Mag, The Cornfield Review,* and the *Olio* zine. He has also received the 2020 Lyric Prize for OSU Marion students. He got introduced to poetry through competitive slams.

He still exercises his enjoyment of performance poetry at Kafe Kerouac where Wednesday readings have become a sort of ritual. His high school teacher, Dr. Jones and the Columbus native, Hanif Abdurraquib, are his biggest influences in writing.

ALLIGATOR BAIT IN REVERSE

Look!
Look how the wiggling bodies eject
From the water, the murk and the dirt cannot tension
Their bleeding souls, they explode
From the surface as aviators. The liquid teeth
Beading on their skin, arms swooping towards a buoyant heaven,
Great webbed fingers like wings

Look!
Look how free they slide, gliding
In the puffed blue, disrobed of a god's conscience.
Their joy jaunts the water's haunting,
They slant like firework streaks
Leaving loud screams as vapor trails

Look!
Look how forgiving this map is when you hold it
Upside down—Look!
It's almost as if the world wears Africa like a crown
Like it was never an upturned bucket of flesh dumping brown
Bodies into the sea of the new world.

I walk past

Another city of hopes learning homelessness
Outside the metropolitan library,
Bracing. It is the security guard's voice that is the loudest—
Firm and quiet—stuffed full of regret,
I know I wouldn't have the heart to reintroduce someone to a street
I know would never love them back,
Leave them to court the bench for a night,
Asking for a dance of their dreams.

These vague shapes have endless pouches.
Bags within bags within bags of nothing.
Capable of carrying all of us. A span from the harassment of night
To the rejection of an upturning tomorrow
To the disgust crumpled on the faces of the showered.
The detritus a downpour; all we give
Collected like gift wrap for a vagabond
On the wind

WITH ENOUGH BLOOD AND MONEY

Anyone can be white. Anyone can be
Safe as an assumption, like hunchin'
In the back of a Saab
In an alley off the shadows of High Street

Anyone can throw the clay of a morning into a wanted poster
Like all these LLCs are looking out for me,
    Like take a number from the mustache'd strip and start tomorrow,
Like you need to be here
On time, but trust traffic is in no rush at all

With enough dying,
Any town's graveyard can grow to host a golf course.
Any self respecting player knows the greenest grass is on the other side of the Tombstone, that
soil, is the filthy richest,
But rain can spoil
A productive vacation day

See how pretty
The old iron in the river running red at the bottom,
With enough change
In your pocket, you can float at any sea level,
Sit in the lake investment, saturated,
The undercurrent takes its time ripping Ty and Patricia apart
For the algae to bloom

Isn't it funny how everything just keeps getting greener?
Isn't it lovely how everything dark keeps getting deeper?

MY DAD SINKS A BOAT

I didn't know Hell
was just rain;
How much I hate
my need for heat,
blood-soaked, like batter-dredge
but never fried– Just sopping, sopping,
sobbing.

And I wonder what
I thought heaven was–
Smirking in the reflection
of clouds surrounded by no one,
yet not ever alone, not ever
searching for another body to cry for,
only looking down on everyone that is drowning.

GRANNY'S HOUSE GOLD STANDARD

Of course that is and always will be; The cork tan of the sidewalk
Gasping under unemployed sneakers bleached by the sun

Is another world to the oasis of lawn
Untouched by sons of guns
Who spread their evenings over cracked bud lights

It's not that you have to be alone, just, in this refuge,
Not one impression of red Solos
Or alley cats scrapping over the offspring of catcalling and hips shaking
Could last through the threat of jail.
The bars on granny's door
Are a cage, that
Shhhhhlept - clap!
Of the screen door is the yawn of a lion

To me, Granny is as large as the house.
To me, her paw could bat the moon,
I wish this oasis stretched the length of the world
And became an ocean

I imagine a pail as large as my Granny's hands
Scooping into the sea
Scrubbing every biome until
No man would ever dare put a toe in

BACK AND FORTH

Like a Cameo song, Death rocks to the rhythm
Of souls that he sweeps low to the earth
They're easy on their knees, praying on Death's
Row, like overgrown willow trees, their pleas
Grow louder against the concrete, and Death as jolly
As can be, jingles his keys, whistling with a baton beat
Like cleaning house, early in the morning,
Like throwback jams that wake you up to fabuloso
And lawn mowing. I believe that a man that puts another man
To death is something like an "All-Knowing"
Because the court date for the spring execution
Is the nickname of rebirth, unlocking the cell
To an afterlife, to a chorus of new birds chirping, elongating their
Throats for the new grain in their homes.
I'm saying the new grain built your homes,
Built the foundation under all that earth,
Built with the seeping chlorophyll,
Fading to black among the melee of Other,
Growth thrown into mortar, sewed like thread into the fabric
Of every home. Who knows
How many more screams
Should be cut, to keep the lights
On.

AMELIA CHRISTMAS GRAMLING
Bowling Green, Kentucky

is a graduate from the University of Iowa's Nonfiction Writing Program and the recipient of Iowa's Postgraduate Provost Fellowship. Amelia is an educator and writer from southern Kentucky. She believes in harnessing the traditions of documentary poetics and creative nonfiction to investigate, preserve, and even resurrect that which binds us to the landscapes we call home.

To map a river

1.

To map a river,
you begin
at the ending
and turn
upstream

2.

past
cinderblock trailers,
two-by-four stilts,
homes suspended
in the image
of the wind.

No promise
or pretense
of weather-
ing the weather.
Every home in southern Mississippi
was built
to bend.

We do not stop
for Gator Den,
Nor Patchatoula, not
Tick Faw, or
Apocalypse-
Sports:
Ammunition
Surplus
Store

It's 70 degrees
in January.
The passenger's-side window is collecting steam.
Stars I finger-painted
on my breath
this New Year's Eve
are returning.

The mid-day moon, risen, is another
ghost-
ly body,
a premonition peeking through a memory.

3.

A bald eagle heads South in September.
He flees the Yukon
where winter is half the year.

The river is
his map,
his nose, the compass.
A delicate instrument, it detects
the thin scent of thaw
from an aerial distance.

(On the road, we're in a bigger rush.
We rise
& winter takes 12 hours
to catch us.)

A scavenger, he'll hunt
carp if he can get them.
But a vole will do in a pinch.
His thrift's a habit leftover from leaner seasons.
He has the instinct—if not the memory—
of skimming
extinction.

Spotting his
down-belly
in a glassy lake
is still an event,
a ghost sighting
himself.

Close cousin,
after all
to the growing canon
of creatures
gone

to live
a second, thinner life
as art.

At the southern border of Iowa, he shows off,
swooping low over a stream
of traffic.

Inside
two right feet
go down hard.

(The driver pumps the brake
while I provide the sound effects.)

The eagle's resurrection is alarming
for its exception.
Ours is a species better suited to emergency
than preservation.

4.

Monday-Friday I
step past a gaggle
of EMTS
dispatched to the river
to rescue the same man

who is not drowning.

the white-capped swimmer
from California
is however
draining
tax dollars & patience.

He doesn't look endangered,
but you'd have to have a death wish
to get in this water
(or so report
the 911 callers).
Bodies, though,
are easy to spot when they surface
at the base of the flood-control dam.

In the Midwest, a river frozen-solid
is often a ruse.
Under a skin of ice, a current
runs
all year.

5.

Dusk comes early
to the last exit.

The sky stoops
to meet or be eaten
by corn &
wheat stalks-sharp
ened
on relentless interstate speeds

I am sleeping

& wake
to the color of emergency
turning the distance
blue-red-red.

You want to see a bird graveyard?
Asks the president's voice
on the 10:00 news repeating
a 6:00 story
Go under a windmill.
You'll see more birds than you've ever seen
ever
in your life.

6.

The new restaurant
in the old power plant
is only troubled by ghosts, says the owner,
occasionally.
They aren't mean. But they do things
at inopportune times.
They turn out lights
and call out

my name. They spread mist.
But they never tamper with the food.
No appetite.

Patio-seaters delight in a view of the footbridge
& flood-control dam,
geese, ducks, and even
bald eagles
if you can white-knuckle
the winter-chill
in the off season.

7.

When the rains come
we'll pack only as much as will fit in the trunk,
buoyed by what the mayor said.

So much can be replaced.

A new city hall,
a new city water system,
a new city river gauge to provide more accurate forecasts
from here on
out.

So much can be replaced.

8.

Battery-powered
candles
make the vigil easy to spot
from the bridge.

A body has been dragged from the river.

The Dean of Students
can't explain
what he doesn't remember.
It's true of any age,
ours especially.

To be young is to live

in a State
of Emergency.

We don't need to make sense of this tonight.
So, let's raise our
lights.

9.

The end of the river
is the same as the beginning,
either way, a mouth.

He says *picture it*

& I picture a grave
the size of New Jersey,

but metaphors made on land
don't hold their shape
in the water:

"grave" for instance.

To call something dead
it must once have been living,

and the Dead
Zone off the coast
of Mississippi
is devoid
of the possibility
of possibility

including growth.

And yet it's growing
a little every year, fed

on run-off
from a river
in a landlocked state
whose corn outweighs its people
in the electoral count.

I know this,
and yet I don't feel it to be true -
the weight -
when the river rises (at least once a day)
to blind me
through the rearview
window.

This is the difference, I wager,
between people and eagles.

Our distance from a fact doesn't change
no matter how far we travel.

TERRY HERMSEN
Delaware, Ohio

is Professor Emeritus of English at Otterbein University. He has published four books of poems, including *The River's Daughter* and *A House for Last Year's Summer*, along with *Poetry of Place: Helping Students Write Their Worlds* (NCTE, 2009). He has taught poetry for Ohio Arts Council in over 100 schools, along with EECO's Language of Nature workshops at Cuyahoga Valley Environmental Education Center. He has led "poetry night hikes" in several state parks around Ohio, Vermont, and California. Since 2017, Terry has sought to bring together climate change initiatives across colleges in central Ohio. In August of 2021, he released an album of climate/earth songs entitled "Dance Floor at the Edge of Time," which he has performed in Cleveland, Columbus, Bluffton, and Sandusky in Ohio, as well as in Kentucky, Indiana, Maryland, Vermont and the University of Iowa.

THE SMALLEST RIPPLE

And now the island pauses as, from the boat,
it disappears.

As the sky turns, as the waves lip and swallow.

The light bends, they say, in wren's eye
or Palomar, the shadow of us aching with all
we must deflect.

If I could I would lie deep inside the morning
as if it were a sea.

Each day the smallest ripple.

The traitor's exile is his desert home: garden
on a cliff, ladder for a door.

Dark expanse to train the heart to story.

The eldest stories trouble the edge
where summer borrows back
its liquid calendars.

No end to how the mountains whisper,
blow up a storm four bands of blue.

The man who climbs this day a ladder
folds up his house, all his grief

held together by the winds.

Sugar Maple

Far from the voices, the tree pulls me up
   into its gray evolving spiral. Here nothing need be proved,
   only the wide July day, thick with ants,

   their homes in the roots, their curious persistent highways
   up the trunk. Out in the meadow, pairs of goldfinches, like clipped
   and undulating pulsating flames

   light on the gritty thin strands of coneflowers, adding
   hardly a sway as they pluck the heads clean
   like tiny Russian hats, leaving rows

   of dark indentations, continuous sentences in braille
   repeating all one word. For the finches the heights I've climbed in an hour
   would hardly be the thrust of two

   incantations. Oh why then not stay
   up here? I've walked all the melodies, held open
   the door for love, trimmed my face

   in the mirrors till it's thin as a fan, melted
   the eyes of candles, turned the columns
   of the glassy sandstone cities. Here

   my arms are long and supple, multiple as some
   Midwestern Shiva, my evil columns entwined with their redemptive
   silhouettes, no head but this dark stubbly

   phylum flowing skyward
   and rootward, at least a half of me
   webbed below the ground, so heart-hollow

   I can feel my limbs 20 feet or more in all directions
   ride each small breeze, shift for a furious
   and sudden rain, hardly a drop winding its way down

   to my ghosted inner ground.
   A wildfire could sweep this meadow
   and I would still stand, singular and scarred, recording that summer

   like a knife in my bark I'd slowly curl
   my bulk around. But here, nearly invisible, a doe

edges a few feet from my calm

drip circle, with her twin fawns who nuzzle
the dark promise between
her thighs. I don't scare her

with my humid, human breath
now as still as hers, now nearly
as eternal.

THE GREEN MAN   *(a circular/reversible poem)*

Wandering the third floor shelves : *The Green Man*—
with headshots some scholar-photographer tracked one summer
in a grant across the gray cathedrals. Within the schema
of the great grand buttresses, admittedly a minor motif writ large
through her season's camera: dry mask within a cornice—all that weight
above—spews oak leaves out of his eyes, or grows the forest
like some swollen proclamation from his beard, sprouts
the thick of a vine from a furrowed forehead, stalk
burst through the skin. The 14th-century's fear of earthly bondage—
distant memory where our faces—or our gods—grew in the leaves. Bacchus
or the Lionhearted, or some wayward apostles'
severed heads bowed home again—as if the forest itself
were a chorus and thrust these stone or wooden eyes
into arching, antiphonal hymns. As the many angels with their scales
for weighing our grief. From drunken longings,
layered faces, skulls of resurrection
and descent, emergent massive
coiling heads, set beneath all that stone
here, a grinning sot, there a scarified warrior,

for centuries lodged in the niches
the joints and cornices
from which entanglement is spun:
green face carved into gray stone
ceaseless as birdsong, sourceless
as mushroom, silhouetted to the ageless rite,
let us climb back in
cantilever of wayward
looming branches,
fierce-born fever
of the bearded glance,
solitary sentry
whose eyes say
nothing as they
bore into us,
across the pool
of carved years,
all their carvers gone
into the looming
arches of the world,
hidden blessings
over doorways,
seasons we've forgotten
how to name:
what praise do you intend
with leaves woven
for ears, moments
convicted into vine
and song, high
inside the choirs:
green man whose
shame we must now
borrow, conjured Christ
of the endless birth,
surging resurrection of
swollen earth—
put on your garment

Snail along the Allegheny Trail

Steep descent into this ghostly town
  where the ghostly limbs of Pennsylvania Oil
          and Quaker State refineries still scar
  the flats along the river bend : in Emlenton, ferns
              grow twenty feet from the Allegheny Trail
    and the fence warning visitors away
from its lost industrial glory. Now winter runners
  jog where stacks burst slag, a tiny stem

roots in a coagulated chunk of char, a snail
  stretches out its translucent neck
            to cross the asphalt. It's Thanksgiving
    and I am on my way along Route 80
            to eat the feast of hospital potatoes
    with my sister and her daughter
and her husband of a year. Two tumors
    have been excised from her brain. She cannot place

the two of clubs upon the ace, nor sense nor see
  the wall before her stumbling steps
          but we will toast this day
    and whatever days emerge from her
            long tunnel. Underneath the ground I know,
      through most of Pennsylvania, crews are blasting
massive streams of hydrochloric acid,
    diesel fuel and any other blend

of chemicals and blind ego they can find
  to stir a last hurrah from the Marcellus shale
          you rest upon, dear Emlenton,
    and that my sister sleeps upon.
          I'll sing her "Simple Gifts,"
            that Shaker hymn, and we'll imagine a valley of delight.
For now, the sun breaks through
    a heart-shaped bole in an oak high on the riverbank,

crews from Texas, Oklahoma, crowd the holiday
  motels along the turnpike, and all the streams
          that feed the Susquehanna, Black Fork and your cold
      gray river spinning its slow circles round this bend
                await the taste of brine. I kneel
        in the leaves, the snail curls to my touch, the runners,
circling back,   thud the trail with their hulking sound,
    the chunk of slag in my winter pocket thrusts up a small green hand.

GOLDFINCHEW WITH MEADOW

for Susie—in remission

                    Goldfinches weave
        the living heights   in and out of pines
        the oaks that name   and us—call us
      the pines, the aspen,   to our perch above
            winds to stir   the meadow, teach us
      bring us a dozen   the questions
      or imitate union,   of sleep and days,
        midair, mid-July   the random play
    and detection. Mate   of cards and discontent,
  for moments from flight   cures and illusion.
        like them, hidden   They undulate,
                yellow leaves   and in a tree
              with scattered

from FIVE DAYS AT THE END OF THE WORLD

1

Place the wind on a post and spin it, like those children's games where
you cannot reach the ball passing and gyrating over your head. So here
the world draws in its air, as Christian says, breathing in a wild rotation.
I move slow, a frail letter, like a candle or a sail trying to burn upright
or at least not drown. The wind is blind and I am deaf. I watch the signs
for how to smile, or not, for all the *pasajeros* holding on in the winds to
the wires of the world.

2

Greg blames it all on *los humanidades*, each crowned scholar scrambling
for life in a little hole in that grand tree, holding on with pickaxes and well-
trained teeth. Look at the world on fire down below, the overturned cars,
the tight hearts of twin explosions, the children gunned down with their little
backpacks on. But here we are eating our Greek scrolls, baked with dusk,
here is the thick jam of theory to make palatable the grit of the bones.

3

Rafael is buying bananas today, far off in Santiago, because tomorrow he
will feed the orphans cereal and toast for breakfast and guide them through
their games. He wants me to feel the words of his faith, walking them for me
forward and backwards. Sometimes he falls into them like a welcoming bed,
he says, tracing a cadence that balances him through the deaths. For me, he is
Alyosha, the brother who wants to bring this Ivan close to the fire. I hold up
the words of his book from this far away and try to touch their scars as they
flare down the tunnel.

5

Habits of exile : even in the Castillo del Diablo, they channel smiling
songs. It is a trick, of course. You cannot tell the devils from the kind.
That is the burden of exile at the end of the world. There are no tides,
no play of time. Plastic trinkets appear on tombs. The girl soldier at 25
has been taken into the arms of El Señor. You wander through ghosts.
It is the Day of All the Saints. They paint the houses for the dead again.

8

On the Day of the Dead, the eyes of Magellan wake on his pedestal beside
his expansive Strait. They are still aghast at their bright and frightening luck,
that this channel may lead to glory. How many villages across the Pacific
would he have to burn to show the power of Christ, armor, swords and
cannons to impress the recalcitrant kings? Can he see his own death, three
months away from his bronze visage, the 500 years it will take to spread the
local wars around the world?

9

And why have I come all this way from my own dead to honor faces I have never seen? I trail the military band, the pride of Los Bomberos. By evening the secondary city outside the walls continues on. The festive tents, mechanical monkeys, sausages, balloons. And here, the seller of daffodils, which Luis loves because of Shelley's poem, which by next winter will sink into their graves, will wait for the crush of swirling, invasive winds, at the end of the world, to open their hearts.

10

Now the graves are empty. From my window I watch them pour into the streets and what can I do but join them. Fallen from the ship-that-is-now-monument, they unfold from their black plastic inside of which they have learned again to breathe. The naked daughters of the Yamana run with me over the cliffs, their breasts swaying below the tides, gathering crabs. I live in caves, Darwin mocks me and brings a frame to measure my illusions. In the Forest of the Winds, I open flags of fire. In the Port of Hunger, I mount a cannon to claim the throat of the seas.

12

And who will I visit here if the world is now filled, Father of the Spiral House borrowed from the snail, Mother of the Seas, Sister Whose Songs Escape Me every day? I am a sail and a candle still, two wheels following the knife edge of the Strait. The Disappeared remain so, but there is no grave that does not hold their names, and no stone anywhere where I must not bow down.

HANNAH STEPHENSON
Columbus, Ohio

is the author of *Cadence* (winner of the 2016 Ohio Chapbook Prize from the Wick Poetry Center) and *In the Kettle, the Shriek*; she also served as series co-editor for *New Poetry from the Midwest* (in 2014, 2017, and 2019). Her writing has appeared in *The Atlantic, The Huffington Post, 32 Poems, Vela, SWWIM, The Journal, Verse Daily,* and *Poetry Daily*. You can visit her online at The Storialist (www.thestorialist.com).

SHOO

What is kindness What is niceness
trying to alleviate

Ball of barbed wire
rolled downhill and neutralized

thorns embraced by morsels of mud
One is better

Both are true but
one is truer and often more difficult

There are mousetraps and poison
holding firm a soft

small body choking
the movement from it with a little

subtlety to make a room nice Let us
not fool ourselves

Nothing kind in this
This is entirely different from the man hired

by my sister to encourage the raccoon
to walk away willingly

from her attic Shoo
Scram please He cuts a temporary hole

into the wall A door He will reseal it
after the raccoon leaves

This is kindness This
and what he does with his dog along rivers

Once a week they drive out to geese who
mistake water and grass

amid cars and roads for
safety He parks the car opens the door

and out comes the dog barking chasing
a toothless warning

A predator lives here
Please keep your feathered body alive

far away from us Even though we love
to feed what flies

SWAP PLACES

Whoever's dreamscape this is please speak up
and claim it or I'll assume it's reaching out
for my hand Lake that is beautiful who
do you belong to Green-tressed hills do
you have a parent to collect you Every lovely
place feels like it has called me and now I
am picking it up from school Mother wheeling
from home to fetch it All of this is what I
imagine when really it's the land who must
see me as the infant barely here in any
experience So few-seasons-wise to feel
wise Baby within me now I know your name
because your dad and I chose it
and when the snow comes you'll be here
One day we will swap places honey
It will be you who is out here
in the grass which hauls itself up above
the ground as it always has and it'll be me
who is not here Please don't feel afraid my son
This is nothing more than leapfrog

STANLEY'S BOWL

Every spring my husband and I discuss
the long-dead animals in the Cadbury commercial
running since we were kids: pig, cat, lion, turtle,
bunny. The wrong animals audition
to become the clucking bunny. This is the American
symbol of Easter, which I didn't grow up with,
except for jelly beans and chocolate. (When my father
was a boy he would use a chocolate bunny's head
as a goblet for his milk.) Instead I had the ten plagues,
parsley dipped in saltwater, buttered and salted matzoh,
opened door. Judaism is all about the symbols
and the stories and the food and the funny-sad. The minor key.
The tragic violin and exuberant clarinet, the klezmer absurd.
Vegetarians, my family put a Milk-bone on our seder plate.
The Passover seder is the story of enslavement and then freedom,
and never forgetting that there were those who hated us
from whom we had to flee. And that when oppressors die,
we must not rejoice in their human pain. Sure, sure,
but who wouldn't cheer as tyrants fall, as the waters
whale-gulp them down. Saltwater means tears, food is a story
of survival, and parsley means the green coming back to the yard.
The seder means, Here is who hated us and tried to kill us
and here we are still. Now, my sister chops apples and nuts,
brings the haroset in the yellow bowl that Stanley, our terrier,
once ate from. He's there, just outside my dad's kitchen,
our perennial digger and yard escapee, thief and planter of dolls
whose miniature limbs would protrude from the dirt, the tiny undead.
Stanley sleeps under the yard and not alone, long ago buried
and returning to us with the trees and grass and apples and spring.
We will not forget. I will not forget Charna, my grandma's spunky friend,
jovial baker of mandel bread, and how she had survived the camps.
Grinning, she divulged to me and my sister how she told
the Nazis to their faces that they needed more food, thicker soup,
and her demands were met. What did she give up in negotiating this,
and what did she earn, a secret skeleton of steel and courage and love.
We also learned that the women fashioned and passed around
a bloody menstrual pad as protection, to try to ward off rape
by crafting the guards' disgust. What seeds existed in her
that nudged her to ask Nazis for anything, to scavenge fabric
and blood and deliver it from woman to woman, clutched and folded,
a love letter, a ballad about generosity and pain, lantern-bright.
Where does this bravery in the midst of horror

come from, and how can we get more. Why is this night
different from all other nights, a question we ask ourselves
every year, when we should ask, How is this time different
from all other times, how is this agony different from other agonies.
When someone suffers, the Jew also suffers,
says the Passover story. And we want this to be true.
But between suffering and safety, there is a heavy door.
Closed. On this side, we eat apples and chocolate
and eggs full of candied yolk and drink simulated tears.
On the other side, all we can barely look at or hold in our
minds, the flame-ravaged house we could be chased from,
the thirst and loneliness of the exiled, the small hands
reaching up from yard's cold mud that we see silhouetted
in the twilight and call broadleaf, dollarweed, thistle.

Also me

[reaches into poem and plucks *me* out, like a dandelion]

[too many ways to start a story]

[too many beautiful non-stories to carve out and point to, saying, here is the cave's entry and exit]

[discovers mothering shifts one's rhetorical situation entirely]

[recalls being in labor, and not being able to smile at the nurses speaking kindly to her, that this is one of the first times she cannot trade pleasantries with other people, she can only breathe in this place where the rope coiled around her torso is wrenched in opposite directions]

[within her, an immense gratitude smolders]

[starts again, looks for the right opening]

[considers the tan and green-tinged whirlybirds winging down from the maples over her and toddler son]

[knows toddler son's name might as well be the first line of every poem now]

[reads own poems from before son was born, curiously, gazing from behind her own former shoulder]

[the body is context and landscape, convex, concave]

[what falls from trees is punctuation]

[declares that the day has a narrative arc, calls this morning and this lunch and this an afternoon stroll]

[recalls placing baby son into stroller, carting him around the block. Then wearing baby son strapped to chest. First, little round face pointed toward her body, ice cream in a cone, then facing out, legs pumping like a fast-forward cuckoo clock]

[admires the sturdy efficiency of toddler's small body, helps toddler walk out the door and off he goes, toddling. Watches him seek and collect headless dandelions, sticks, rocks]

[hears the slap of a basketball meeting asphalt in the neighbor's backyard, where the visiting-from-college son plays on the scaled-down court his father built for his seventh birthday]

[sees her toddler stomp and slowly spin in pollen and tree detritus, exclaiming, *Wheeeee!*]

[lets exclamation mark stand, despite apparent dislike of question marks and most periods]

[remembers that period has not yet returned since before pregnancy, is fine with this, notes it, brushes the thought away like an eyelash from a cheek]

[walks as always with the toddler toward the pine on the corner, crunches brown pine needles and tree parts, toddler reaching for pinecones, bark, ants]

[is directed by toddler on walks now, is utterly without hostility about this. He is the compass needle drawn by his own volition, he steers and she clears the path for him, redirects]

[tells son, *We do not eat rocks, yucky yucky, Let's not eat dirt, makes us sick, We don't walk through other people's grass and yank their flowers from the ground*]

[knows *favverfavverfavver* is his way to say flower, pointing, with urgency]

[wonders what will he think of her when he is older, imagines him saying to someone across a table, coffee cup almost to his lips, *Well my mother was like this, my father was like that…*]

[knows that there is so much beyond this neighborhood this morning this story, that this cul-de-sac is sacred and privileged and limited, a pouch clasped shut but leaking]

[sees dandelions and thinks, weeds]

[sees dandelions and thinks, colonists]

[sees dandelions and thinks, all flowers are colonists]

[sees dandelions and thinks, I am a colonist but I don't wish to be]

[sees dandelions and thinks, colonization and persecution is in my blood, as is being colonized and persecuted]

[sees dandelions and thinks, nature is not living metaphor]

[to make a metaphor, knows a human is needed]

[gives toddler headless flower, just a stem, and looks on as he adds it jubilantly to the three crumpled in his small fist]

[believes that each day is the start of a new season, each day a new word, five new words, a new ability, expression, interest]

[knows that later she will look out her bedroom window, into the biggest beyond, moon-seeking. As she looks for it every night, while her boy sleeps in his own starstrewn bedroom, while downstairs her husband watches a basketball find hands and gravity and halo hundreds of times while the seconds drip down to zero]

[lets the moon tell her that there is no start, no ending, just points of light]

JERK

Does the flower feel any any horror
I imagine that the flower can only feel rapture
or contentment

The ridiculous human
thinks about how flowers cannot communicate

Meanwhile one flower is telling every flower in the park
Hey everyone, check out this poor jerk

And that flower can share this
with every flower that has ever lived
in or near this soil

And the bee can carry flowerlanguage
And leaves hear your heart
Plants practice what their life will be
once you have joined them

This will be easy
Do not be scared of your breaking pieces

This is the message clinging to the foot
of all bees

DEAL

Tug the fur over your skin,
hide your old head with your new one.

Be the bear that traps humans.
Be the shouting man.

Go to the snow for courage.
Fill your jaws with sharper teeth.

Already, you are moving differently.
See how you've taken to slouching,

skulking. Ruin the snow as you move
so you can be followed. Find a cave

where the snow won't blow in,
begin forgetting words, blot out

all gentility, and I will track you there.
Only wildness can comfort you.

FAIRY TALE

Long ago, magic swam through tree roots
and rivers and stones. Science slumbered

underground, a hidden well. The woods
were the place where life happened, slowly,

or the field with the woods nearby, visible.
Even hundreds of miles away, sixteen towns

over, the same woods. A little house there,
within the woods, criss-crossed branches

above that do not block out the sun. Garden,
shaded rooms, white curtains like hands

accompanying a voice saying *I don't know,
could be that, could be this*. Then the family,

beginning in kindness and love, a daughter
of a farmer, a boy with an axe and candle.

There is a baby coming to them, working
her way through the underside of the world,

untidy with thickets of thorns. When she
gets here she will have to learn how to live

without every being she will come to love,
her father and mother, the lambs, the sparrow

she heals. The magic helps her find food,
but cannot make the dead return. There are

arrows and there is poison. The hardest part
is leaving the seed in the ground to see

if the magic will work. You have to forget
it is out there. The dark forest can keep you

safe at night. Let the dirt pull at what hurts
you. You came here for this pain.

Microclimates

(for Avery)

In the car
on the bridge
in the fog
that holds the city like time
made thick and visible

In the week before my children
begin school
in the trenches of my beloved friend's
heartbreak

I think of how we cannot contain
ourselves
How in being here longer
we get brittler and more permeable

narrative passing and dispersing through us
atomized
oil and fragrance spraying from the skin
of a clementine being opened

If only I could smell like a clementine
being peeled nearly whole
coating the **hands** of my peeler with the memory
of the taste

Blood orange
Satsuma
Tangerine

This is the story I chase through perfume
The story I try to claim as my own
That what is bitter can be removed cleanly
That there is sweetness in being undone

In the crisp air of the open window
in the chill of August
that my mind brays at
behind our masks that hold our breath in close

on Saturday morning
in the year two thousand and twenty one
on the burning fraying rock
that has nowhere to run from its own destruction

I claim this enclave for a beige mug of coffee
I claim this corner seat and friendship
Those trees
mine
and these thickened palms
craning their necks over the pathway here
watching us walk beneath them in arboreal kindly detachment

Their gossip sounds like
the ocean going psssssh

Yesterday on the windblown beach
we watched a man and woman posing
for wedding photographs
looking out over the waves
White dress and veil and hair and bouquet and sand wild around them
a dust devil

The photographer yelled over the wind and water to to the bride
Turn this way! Let your flowers drop!
Veronica, let the flowers drop!

And as she looked back toward the beach
toward the camera
away from the water
and lowered the flowers
the wind
the light
the veil
composed themselves around her in an instant

Let them drop, Veronica
That's it
Turn and face the wind

AUTHOR COMMENTARIES:
Poetry in a Time of Crisis

CHRISTIAN FORMOSO

[NOTE: In the excerpt below, Christian Formoso, born and raised along the Strait of Magellan, reflects on the legacy of what has been called "the discovery" (sic) of that Strait, which occurred 500 years ago in 1520, taking it as something of a metaphor for the international experience of European colonialization—and calling for a new envisioning of history.]

Gaston Bachelard maintains that only landscapes we've previously seen in dreams do we look at and live with passion. And because the landscape of dreams is the deepest material of our harvest, this Strait and its shores have been part dream, part transit and part destiny, lived with passion by those who have sewn and offered their gaze to the limits of life and the extremities of the south. Chaos and calm, coming and going of an endless journey, the history of our Strait and of our great navigators in boats and canoes, with their stumbling and deeds and tragedies, baptized or anonymous, written or oral, known or forgotten, did not begin 500 years ago. We will not find the depth of these waters and their metaphors as long as we do not coin a more vast, luminous and inclusive memory, to open ourselves to a plural consciousness of our stories. No, all the while we go on carrying the same old meanings of the maps and the echoes of imperial disillusionment, and the dominant ways of seeing and seeing ourselves in Magellanes.

[…] It would be necessary to seriously hoist and fill with a new meaning—new because unprecedented—the fullest depth of our dreams and our symbols. All the borders that we have learned and to which we have clung should finally be revealed to us for what they are: scars, seams that in an ultimate sense call for crossing and embracing.

JEFF GUNDY

Poetry changes nothing, Auden famously wrote. And yet, he added, "it survives, / A way of happening, a mouth." Caught up in the many troubles and disasters of our times, it's easy to dismiss poetry, and all of the forms of action available to us, to sink into gloom as the terrors and destruction drive onward, and so many in our nation and across the world seem positively, gleefully dedicated to damaging other people and the planet in any way they can. This is not new, but it does seem worse than usual.

Not accidentally, the backlash in this country that threatens so many basic rights—even, it seems the right to live on a planet that will sustain human life—has come when suppressed voices of all sorts are finally speaking out, demanding seats at the table and voices in the long struggle toward human and worldly flourishing.

Old white guys like me find ourselves in an odd place. People in our demographic have done, and continue to do, so much damage, even while some of us have mourned and called out and done what we could to resist for most of our lives. It wasn't enough—

that's plain now—but what next? Just get out of the way, give over our space in the public conversation to those long-silenced and suppressed? That's happening anyway, to some degree, and fair enough. But is that enough?

Anyone not frustrated and dismayed by the state of the world is either crazy or not paying attention, as far as I can see. Those of us privileged with some time and money have the chance and the obligation to use those resources to try, at least, to shift the world toward survival, to tug against the vast inertia of history. Words are not powerful in the way of missiles and artillery shells, but artful creations have shifted the course of things before, and maybe, just maybe, they can do so again.

I'm writing this on the Fourth of July, that irony-suffused holiday. My Mennonite ancestors mostly sided with the Tories or just tried to stay out of the rebellion, citing the verse that calls for Christians to be subject to the authorities. Now it's not at all clear that even the flawed, semi-representative government we've lived under will survive for long.

I'm of the newer school of Mennonites who believe that Jesus calls us to work for justice and peace, and to resist government actors that violate those things. Thomas Jefferson, flawed as he was, found that the right set of words at the right time could kindle a great change. We are all of us flawed, but that is not what matters most when we are working for change. To find the words that will make some kind of key, and the lock that the key fits, and somehow together to find the strength to turn the key and open the door… even now, friends, we must stay together and keep trying. The rest, as old man Eliot says, is not our business.

DIONNE CUSTER EDWARDS
What can a poem offer the fate of this world: a rethreading of the breath of sky and land and water? What can the shape of a line and letters invent in the open mouth of a page: a note to our present and future selves about fierce and urgent matters, a pleading, dangling at the hem of our own existence. The poem is a feather-like depth circling joy and disaster, a pressing on the heart and skin. Perhaps, the erosion is a symptom of our comfort, a resonance of our spoil and mishap. We need a new way to describe the exact spot of wreck and healing. The poem offers a keeping, a breathing archive, a line drawing of a life.

LAUREL ANDERSON
We are in a time of flame. Of flood. Of migration. Of upheaval. Right now, the human body is threatened with new kinds of sickness, extreme heat, drought-related hunger and thirst, and with violence from a society fractured by the pandemic, deep inequalities, political strife, and war. The web of life on Earth is threatened as ecosystems are stressed by human-induced climate change and depleted to support rampant human consumption. As a scientist, poet, and person, I feel like I am scrambling frantically through my brain's tool box to respond to multiple emergencies. My natural science background suggests practical solutions: vaccines, renewable fuels, sustainable farming, water conservation, natural land protections. What does the poet do?

To me, poetry, and the arts in general, have much to offer in this time of global environmental crisis. The first role of the poet is that of unflinching witness. While science can record largescale trends and shifts, it does so as a collective, as a hive mind. We experience the shattering and re-assembly of our world as individuals and remain attuned and responsive to the individual voice. A poem can immerse a person in the experience of the individual, even the imagined experience of a non-human individual, and invite a sharing, or at least a contemplation of that moment. This is vital to forging and re-forging our connections with nature and each other. It is through the individual story that we process the personal consequences of environmental change. Poetry offers gateways into these personal stories and onward into true empathy.

The second role of the poet is to build terrible, wrenching beauty from fear and loss. When we encounter scientific data about the loss of a species, it is presented to our intellectual selves. This is critical because these data are essential to crafting solutions. However, these data also bring about an emotional response—we feel fear and loss. Fear and loss can be paralyzing. These emotions can also lead to violence or despair if people have no outlet for them, or if a society over-focused on rationality ignores them. Poetry sculpts images from fear and loss, calls these feelings real, gives them their place and their due. The work of repair and rebuilding can then truly begin.

For me, as a practicing scientist, the third role of poetry is to connect me to my love for the natural world. I think my work as an ecologist is essential. Indeed, never has the science of ecology seemed so important. Yet, underlying this practical urgency is love. Science has no language sufficiently beautiful and luminous for dogwood blossoms reflected in water, the green glimmer of a beetle, backlit dandelions at sunset, fireflies signaling to their mates, and the way shadows drift under the swaying branches of a willow. Science is hard work. My poetry reminds me why I do this work—it's because I love the natural world. The world needs our love and work the most in times of darkness. Poetry inspires me to take the next difficult step.

TRAVIS MCCLERKING

When it comes to my work, my predominant motivation is the understanding of self. When I write, I am confessing where I have failed at certain points, capturing people that I have been, shading characters that I've played, and painting mental states that I've occupied. They're all the many iterations of myself and I think they are all beautiful. I have been so many people, and they are all beautiful.

Aside from just introspection, I engage heavily in political commentary. In understanding myself, I am required to understand my own placement in history. This is where big picture issues such as climate change and generational wealth weave themselves into my writing. As an only child and the youngest of my close relatives, many of the people that have cared for me have begun to look over to me for comfort; Their memories and lessons live on in me. This is what urges me to conjure a reality that they will likely never get to see; An environment that isn't accosting our bodies through bad actors or pollution. I want to make real a world that addresses our trauma in totality. That, I think, is why my poems often in stride with movements like Afrofuturism. I adopt lenses that allow me to tell the stories of my elders through my young eyes. The poems that I write are new and my own, but they have a familiar wince of pain and a steady rumble of hope that I've acquired through absorbing my family's stories.

AMELIA CHRISTMAS GRAMLING

On the Fourth of July, I attended the memorial service
for a man named Billy Duncan held underneath a lone shade tree at the edge of an
overgrown field in Allen County, Kentucky—a field that Billy had bushwhacked every season
of his life. My story converges with Billy's long before my birth—in 1972 when my father and
eleven of his closest friends moved next door to the Duncan's to begin construction on a
geodesic dome, the primary dwelling for a burgeoning hippie commune called the Flying
Frog Farm. Billy was in '72 as he was at the end of his life, a Kentuckian, born and raised; a
salt-of-the-earth, good old boy, tobacco farmer with a wife and two young children, and in
1972 when the tiny unincorporated community that Billy called home was shocked by the
sudden appearance of eleven unmarried, unwashed, unemployed, long-haired east-coast
college-dropouts who had come to rural Kentucky with ambitions of "living off the land"
despite the fact that not a single one of them possessed any practical knowledge about that
land, Billy did the unthinkable; he taught the hippies how to farm.

Many of those hippies never left. And those that did returned in July to gather
beneath a shade tree and bid their goodbyes to the greatest neighbor they'd ever had.
1972 was post-Manson and post-Kent-State. The culture-war between those that lived by
traditional conservative "family" values and the anti-war, anti-capitalist free-loving youth
movement was raging across middle America, and yet, Billy Duncan did not regard his new
neighbors with mistrust nor hostility. Instead, he offered them a deal—his expertise for their
labor—a trade that, in the months and years to come, would literally save my father's life,
would ensure my brothers would not go hungry, and would keep my family warm during one
of the coldest winters in a hundred years.

I am telling this story today because it contains a lesson that lives at the very
heart of why I write. Nothing—not patriotic duty, not political affiliation, not even religious
doctrine—nothing that Billy Duncan believed in overrode his obligation to his home, an
obligation, that in Billy's eyes, extended beyond what he legally owned and encompassed the
community of which he was a part. In Billy's estimation, he and my father could share nothing
else as long as what they shared was a property line, a water source: in other words, as long as
what they shared was the land.

We live in a time in which the mass injustice, fear, and violence which pushed
my dad and his friends out of the city and back to the land has not abated but is reaching
unprecedented heights. In fifty years, however, human-caused climate change has ensured
that even those with the means to leave have nowhere left to go back to.

To admit that we are irreparably and irrevocably bound to this one dangerous and endangered place; to accept that we are dependent on the generosity of estranged neighbors and
the generosity we extend to neighboring strangers is a distinctly anti-American idea.
And yet the only Americans worth believing in are those who have lived, and died, by that
very belief.

On the fourth of July, my brother, who was Billy's neighbor from birth through college,
stood to pay his respects. He said that the loss had yet to become real for him,
because Billy was so intrinsic to this land, his rhythms so entwined with the seasons, that
for the trees and the fields to remain as they were without him seemed utterly surreal,
impossible. I write to remember a world that has never existed, but still could: where we live
to be remembered by that which remains both before and beyond us, untouched.

TERRY HERMSEN

Writing: little black marks on a page. Connected to tones on the tongue. Or in the throat. And then: somehow connected to the brain. The distance between one stage and the other can be quite far. And then there are our bodies. Where what we call words land. Anxious as we are. Isolate as we are. In currents. Of culture. Of what we call language. In a space. And a time. Ours being a highly endangered one. For us. And so many of the creatures. We share this planet with.

Planet: so separated from words. From this hand. Making lead-embossed marks. On a page. Outside: the tailgate of a van. Smooth mown and edged grass. Around concrete squares. Of sidewalk. Garages for automobiles. Walling off more space. Than our living rooms. Where we welcome in. What moves us. From place to place. No distance too far, no fuel too deep. To not dig up. No matter the heights of the scaffolds. That pound and scrape. What lies below.

What lies below: maybe that's where poems. Come from. Gaston Bachelard has said: "With poetry, the imagination takes its place on the margin, exactly where the function of unreality comes to charm or disturb—always to awaken—the sleeping being lost in automatisms." But how. Do we. Face. The automatisms. Of here? Often for me. And maybe for others. The disconnect is too huge. Our nearly reptilian minds. Vehicles like self-propelled. Behemoths. We ride in. With our minds. And our folded acquiescence.

Poems: non-acquiescence. Beginning here. Wherever we are. Is a place. A strand. To follow. Whatever we love. Might be a guide. Whatever we hunger for. At some deeper level. Than want. Or habit. W.S. Merwin writes about a bee. With its abdomen removed. Gorging on honey it cannot digest. Says: that is us. Poetry: ah, to become the bee. That knows. What's missing. A return. To substance. Versus excess. It's often said that if the rest of the world consumed the amount of resources the U.S. does, it would take four earths to meet the demand. What if. We opened up. Found another time. Looked at each other anew. Looked beyond. Found what might allow us. To begin again.

HANNAH STEPHENSON

I've always seen poetry (my own and others') as a site of play, generosity, possibility. Poems feel like and evoke places. They construct a new way of thinking, moving, feeling, experiencing, and bring you into that space that they're building for you, around you.

Beyond play and delight, I want poems to be a place of protection. But I don't know that they are, or can be. I want them to repair, to shelter, to nourish. Poems (and art) do reach through the misty ether of consciousness into the realm of human life and action, but they aren't cures. They can't prevent people from dying, or stop someone from wielding hate and attacking others, or purify the atmosphere and water we depend on.

I wish poems could turn their tiny, powerful screwdrivers into the heart of all those in power, making adjustments that would restore rights, open borders of our country, erase weapons, keep us safe from ourselves. And maybe they can. From my perspective, poetry is a micro act of goodness and tenderness that can cause ripples, a moment of connection with someone on the other side of the page, on the other side of your own language. We can offer one another kindness, attentiveness, vulnerability. I write toward bravery. I made this for you. And I'm so grateful you're here.

POEMS FIRST APPPEARING IN OTHER PUBLICATIONS

JEFF GUNDY
"Deerflies" (appeared in *Deerflies,* WordTech Editions, 2004)
"Somewhere Near Defiance" and "Additional Assertions on Soul" (appeared in *Somewhere Near Defiance,* Anhinga Press, 2014)
"Contemplation with Ledges and Moon" (appeared in *Spoken among the Trees,* Akron Press, 2007)
"Ambitions" (appeared in *Abandoned Homeland,* Bottom Dog Press, 2015)
"The God of Dirt" (appeared in *Without a Plea,* Bottom Dog Press, 2019)
"The Wind Farm Releases the Wind" (appeared in *Wind Farm: Landscape with Stories and Towers,* Dos Madres Press, 2020)

DIONNE CUSTER EDWARDS
"American History Elevator Pitch" (appeared in *Journal of Cultural Research in Art Education [JCRAE]*).

LAUREL ANDERSON
"Above the River" (appeared originally in *River Heron Review*)
"Willow" "#insectapocalypse. A thread." (appeared originally in *The Fourth River*)
"Climate Change, Ohio" (appeared in an earlier form in *Canary – A Literary Journal of the Environmental Crisis*)

TERRY HERMSEN
Poems in this collection are all from *A House for Last Year's Summer* (Bottom Dog Press, Huron, Ohio, 2017).

HANNAH STEPHENSON
"Shoo" (appeared in *Shallow Ends,* Feb. 2019)
"Swap Places" (appeared in *Cadence,* Kent State University Press, March 2018)
"Stanley's Bowl" (appeared in *Aquifer: The Florida Review Online,* Sept. 2021)
"Also Me" (appeared in *Matter,* May 2018)
"Fairy Tale" (appeared in *io,* May 2014)

Lightning Source UK Ltd.
Milton Keynes UK
UKHW012320171022
410650UK00004B/61